The Knight's Handbook

Claire Llewellyn

Contents

Life as a knight	2
Starting as a page	4
Becoming a squire	6
Fighting fit?	8
Weapons practice	10
Battle dress	12
Horse care	14
Knightly behaviour	16
"Arise, Sir Knight!"	18
The knights' club	20
Knights in battle	22
Tournaments	24
Time to relax	26
Your knightly decision	28
The knights' quiz	30
Glossary	31
Index	32

OXFORD
UNIVERSITY PRESS

Life as a knight

Do you fancy becoming a knight? Do you see yourself in **armour**? Would you like to live in a castle? If you answered yes, yes and yes, then this handbook is for YOU. It explains everything you need to know about becoming a knight.

Who can become a knight?

Most knights come from rich, **noble** families. It's an expensive and dangerous life and the training is long and hard. Though some soldiers are knighted on the spot if they have been brave in battle.

 KNIGHT WANTED

Must be brave and really rich!

Don't even THINK about applying if you are:

- a poor peasant
- not the sporting type
- squeamish
- afraid of danger
- nervous around horses
- keen to live to a ripe old age.

The age of knights

The heyday of knights was in the Middle Ages (from about AD 800–1500). They fought on horseback for the king and were tough and brave.

Knights had to pay for their own armour and horses. This was one of the reasons that it was usually men from rich families who became knights.

Knights' know-how

Women couldn't normally become knights but in 1149 a group of Spanish women were knighted when they defended their town from attack.

Timeline: A knight's lifespan

page
squire
knight
Night, night, knight!

About age 7 | About age 14 | About age 21 | About age 30

That's right, knights had often been killed in battle by the time they were 30.

Starting as a page

If you want to become a knight, you will have to leave home when you are only seven years old. Your parents will send you away to live with another noble family in a great house. It's the start of a new life but don't get *too* excited. You will be taught how to ride and fight but you will also be a servant of the household. You will be a page.

All this bowing can't be good for my back!

Noble truth or fiendish falsehood?

As a page, you must always bow when you approach your lord or lady.

Your **knightly challenge**

As a page, you'll need to serve drinks to your lord and lady. Can you hold a full cup in both hands and present it on bended knee – *without wobbling*?

My Lord Father and Lady Mother,

I am so very tired! I have to get up at dawn each day and help my lord to dress. Then I fetch and carry for my lady. At breakfast, I help to serve at table. After that, I have to learn Latin and French. Later, there are riding lessons. I like them but my horse is stubborn. Yesterday, it threw me and all the other pages laughed. I can't wait until I am a real knight.

Your obedient and loving son, **Oswald**

Pages train together to improve their knightly skills.

Pages exercise a lot to get fit and strong. They train to use weapons, using wooden swords and shields for practice. Sometimes they fight on each other's shoulders to improve their balance and skill.

Becoming a squire

When you reach the age of 14, you'll take the next step in your training and become a squire. A squire is a knight's right-hand man.

Sounds like the perfect job for me!

Wealthy knight seeks SQUIRE

Ambitious 14-year-old lad wanted for friendly household.

Must be strong, hard-working and polite. Must have a taste for adventure. Must be good with horses and an excellent rider.

Main duties: assisting knight and cleaning armour. Will sometimes help to sharpen weapons and work in stables.

We offer a seven-year contract. Full training, food, shared lodging and uniform provided.

Apply to: Sir William Rivers, Bellevue Castle.

Practice makes perfect

As well as being a knight's servant, you must improve your riding and fighting skills. You will spend much of your time reading, writing, drawing, dancing and singing. You must also learn household skills, such as carving meat at the table.

Playing musical instruments like this lute is important to entertain the ladies of the house.

Your knightly challenge

Do you have a song you could sing to entertain the ladies?

I like my meat very wafer-thin.

Fighting fit?

Squires have to be fit, tough and strong. You need to train every day to build your **stamina**, strength and skill.

Top training

Throw the **javelin**.

Fight with long sticks, called quarterstaffs.

Wrestle with other squires.

Run around wearing heavy armour.

Perform **acrobatics**.

Stone put (throw heavy rocks).

Your knightly challenge

Getting fit is hard work. Try running round with a heavy bag on your back.

All this training will help you become a great knight one day.

Games of skill

Squires practise their fighting skills by playing different games. One game is called ring-tilting. Players win points for collecting rings. The smaller the ring, the greater the points!

Knights' know-how

Good knights try not to get hurt. In ring-tilting, they only use lances with blunt wooden tips. They also take care not to poke their horse in the eye and hold their lance upright before and after their run.

How to play

1. **Hang rings of different sizes (2-15 centimetres in diameter) from a tree or stand.**

2. **Mount your horse and tuck your lance under your arm.**

3. **Canter straight towards the rings. Try to catch one on the tip of your lance.**

4. **Turn your horse round to have another go from the other direction.**

Weapons practice

Knights use many different weapons in battle. All of them are sharp and heavy. You will need years of training to know how and when to use them. As a squire, keep all the weapons sharpened and polished so they are ready when your knight needs them!

Sword

The knight's most important weapon. It has hard-cutting edges and a sharp point. Good for striking and blocking blows. The large handle gives a good grip.

Lance

A wooden spear up to 4 metres long, with a sharp iron tip. Always used on horseback. Allows you to attack without getting too close. No good for hand-to-hand fighting.

Club or mace

A heavy metal head on a strong wooden pole. Gives a powerful blow. Strong enough to break a shield.

Battle-axe

A wedge-shaped blade on a short wooden handle. Good for fighting close-up.

Flail

An excellent attack weapon. Its moving ball delivers a heavy blow. Always use very close to your enemy. No good in defence.

Eek! He could really hurt someone with that thing!

Your **knightly challenge**

As a squire, you'll have to polish weapons. Find some old cutlery and polish it until it shines.

Battle dress

One of a squire's most important duties is to dress his knight for battle. Armour can be made from metal rings linked together, called chain mail. Or it can be made from metal plates that cover the entire body.

Under the armour

A knight wears a padded jacket, called a gambeson, and hose (a bit like tights) under his armour.

Hurry up, I'm cold!

Knights' know-how

It's important to put on armour with care. If a single piece drops off in battle, it could cost the knight his life.

Steps to putting on armour

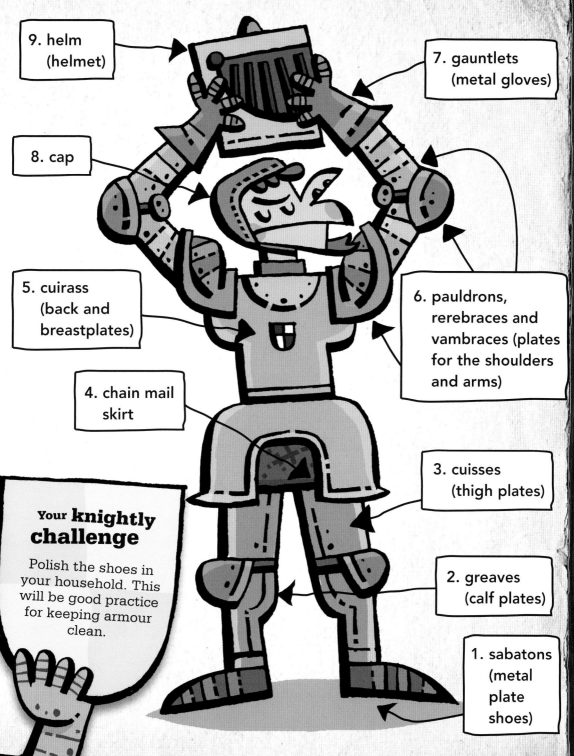

9. helm (helmet)

7. gauntlets (metal gloves)

8. cap

5. cuirass (back and breastplates)

6. pauldrons, rerebraces and vambraces (plates for the shoulders and arms)

4. chain mail skirt

3. cuisses (thigh plates)

Your knightly challenge

Polish the shoes in your household. This will be good practice for keeping armour clean.

2. greaves (calf plates)

1. sabatons (metal plate shoes)

Horse care

Horse care plays an important part in the life of a knight. You must learn to care for them well as they cost a lot of money (twice a squire's annual salary!). You must feed and groom them, **muck** them out and harness them for your knight.

Knights' know-how

Being around horses every day gives squires excellent horse sense. It helps them to become experts at caring for their horses.

Noble truth or fiendish falsehood?

Knights buy armour for their horses to wear.

I deserve more than a carrot for carrying this heavy knight around!

Which horse?

Knights have three kinds of horses. Each one does a different job.

I'm a war horse and the most expensive kind of horse there is. I'm strong enough to carry a knight in full armour. I'm not frightened of the noise of battle and I've been trained to bite and kick.

I'm a riding horse. I'm small, light and fast. Nobles, knights and ladies use me for long journeys because I give the most comfortable ride.

I'm a packhorse. I'm strong but not very fast. I carry armour and other equipment. I'm usually given to squires to ride.

Knightly behaviour

Training to be a knight is not just about riding and fighting. You must also learn to *behave* like a knight. You will need to live by a special set of rules called the Code of Chivalry.

One of the rules was to give money to the poor. This was also known as alms.

The Code of Chivalry

I promise to:
- speak the truth
- be kind to the poor
- protect the weak
- treat ladies with respect
- treat prisoners well
- never attack a knight from behind
- show **mercy** if an enemy surrenders.

Signed ....

Good manners

You also have to behave well in your lord's house. At the dinner table, take care to eat politely. Never scratch your head. Never pick your nails. Never clean your teeth with a knife. You must also never blow on your soup or dip your bread in it. Instead, you must sip it carefully with a spoon.

Your knightly challenge

What do you think is good behaviour? Write your own Code of Chivalry.

It was important for a squire to eat politely to show he could be a top knight.

"Arise, Sir Knight!"

If you work hard, you can become a knight by the time you are 21. If you can afford the horses, weapons and armour, then you'll be ready to be knighted. This is a special **ceremony** performed by a noble lord or even the king.

My knighting ceremony, by Oswald De Vere

The night before the ceremony, I had a bath and put on clean white clothes.

In the morning, I knelt before the king and swore to serve him loyally. He tapped me on the shoulder with his sword and said, "Arise, Sir Knight!"

Father gave me a new sword and a pair of **spurs**. I hope I'll be able to use them soon and prove myself in battle.

When you become a knight, you become an important person. It's rather like joining a special club. It brings you plenty of benefits but you have duties, too.

Benefits of being a knight

Knights are trusted by the king and his lords. They are given land and power over local people. The people work in the fields and pay **taxes** to the knight. The **crops** they grow and the animals they raise make the knight and his family rich.

Some knights didn't treat their people well. Some forced them to pay a lot of money to work the land.

Duties of a knight

Life is dangerous and kings and lords often have enemies. So knights must go and fight for them whenever necessary. If there is trouble on the knight's own land, they must fight to protect the local people.

Noble truth or fiendish falsehood?

When a knight goes off to fight, he leaves his wife in charge of his castle and lands.

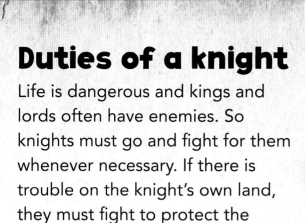

Rather him than me!

I'm out of here!

A knight always defends his castle from attack.

Knights in battle

Knights are expert soldiers who fight for a living. They long to prove themselves in battle and win fame and glory. Before a battle, the knights gather together. At the signal, they grip their lances, spur their horses and charge towards the enemy.

Surviving the battlefield

The battlefield is full of danger. If you are going to survive, you will need your **wits**, courage, strength and luck.

Watch out for metal spikes and wooden stakes stuck in the ground by your enemy.

Listen for arrows flying through the air and protect yourself with your shield.

Friend or foe?

It can be hard to know who you're fighting if your opponent's visor is down. On his shield is his family's coat-of-arms to tell you if he's friend or **foe**.

Your **knightly challenge**

Design your own coat-of-arms.

Symbols

glory and authority →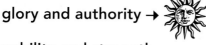

← nobility and strength

safety and protection →

← strength and courage

power and **valiance** →

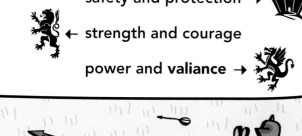

Colours

generous →

← warrior

peace →

← hope

truth →

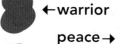

The farmers only have pitchforks and clubs but they are fighting for their lives!

Tournaments

Battles only come along now and then, so how do you keep your fighting skills sharp? One way is to compete against knights in competitions. These are called tournaments and they test your talents in a number of events.

Spring Tournament
Events of the Day

Ring-tilting
Knights compete to spear rings with their lance.

The melee
Two teams fight in a mock battle. Which side will take more prisoners?

The joust
Knights on horseback charge one another. Who can strike their opponent with the lance?

The finale
Awards ceremony followed by a grand feast.

Noble truth or fiendish falsehood?
Armour is so heavy that if a knight falls over he needs help to get up.

The joust

The joust is the main tournament event. Two knights gallop towards each other. They hit each other with their lances. They can win points if they strike a shield or break their lance. They can also score if they knock their enemy off their horse. Blunt weapons are used but there are still injuries. Some knights die from their wounds.

The Castle News

Date: Thursday 24 June, AD1448

SPRING TOURNAMENT

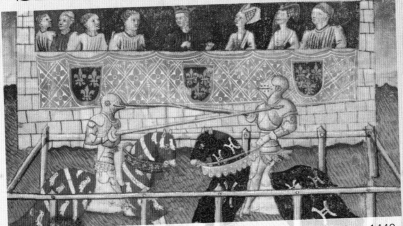

John Chalon of England and Lois de Beul of France jousting, 1448.

The afternoon's joust was a thrilling **spectacle**. There were colourful flags, brave knights in shining armour and brightly-dressed horses.

Nobles and locals cheered on their heroes. All the knights showed great courage but Sir Thomas Hawkwood was the worthy **victor**. He won his enemy's suit of armour.

Time to relax

After all the training and fighting, knights need time to relax and have fun. Perhaps you would enjoy a day in the woods, hunting for deer? Or would you prefer to hunt rabbits and hares with your **falcon**? Remember, hunting isn't just a sport. It provides food for the table.

Knights' know-how

You'll get the best out of your falcon if you win its trust. Hunt with it but also treat it like a pet. Keep it perched on your wrist or chair for several hours a day.

A falcon's brilliant eyesight makes it ideal for hunting small, quick animals like rabbits.

After dinner

In the evening, you will enjoy dinner. Then you and your friends will sing or dance. You might play cards or dice and tell stories by the fire. You will remember the days when you were a squire and had to work from morning till night. Now though, you can just sit back and relax and let your own squire do all the work!

Your knightly decision

Now you know all about a knight's life and the long years of training. So do you still want to be a knight? It's time to weigh up the good and the bad.

You will be rich, live in a castle and have lots of land.

You will have rich and noble friends.

You will enjoy hunting, hawking and feasting.

You will have people working for you.

You will have the chance to win glory in battle.

You will have an adventurous life.

Good points

The knights' quiz

Could you be noble and strong? Could you fight in battle? Take this short quiz to see if you have what it takes to be a knight. Then look on page 32 to see how you scored.

1. You want to become a knight but you are very poor. What can you do to achieve your dream?

a) Impress your local lord by working hard.
b) Beg, borrow or steal the money!
c) Fight bravely as a soldier and hope you are rewarded with a knighthood.

2. Your suit of armour is too heavy to fight in. What can you do?

a) Stop fighting.
b) Remove a couple of the heaviest pieces.
c) Train hard in your armour until you get used to the weight.

3. A battle is about to start. You want to fight on horseback. Which weapon would you use?

a) A mace.
b) A battle-axe.
c) A lance.

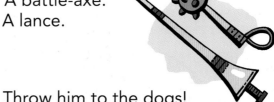

4. You capture an enemy knight. What do you do with your prisoner?

a) Throw him to the dogs!
b) Lock him in the castle dungeon.
c) Keep him under guard in a room in your castle.

5. Your castle and your lands are under threat. What do you do?

a) Ride off to get help from your knightly friends.
b) Arm the people with wooden sticks.
c) Get everyone inside the castle walls and get your soldiers ready.

Glossary

acrobatics   impressive gymnastic movements

armour   metal worn to protect the body

canter   (of a horse) to run gently

ceremony   a formal or public occasion

crops   a large collection of plants that are grown to eat, e.g. wheat

falcon   a bird of prey

foe   enemy

javelin   a light spear

lance   a long, wooden weapon

mercy   forgiveness

muck   dirt

noble   belonging to a rich family with a title, e.g. Lord. It can also be a noun to describe a person from that family.

peasant   a poor farm worker

spectacle   a great performance

spurs   a spiked wheel worn on shoes. The rider presses these into their horse's sides to make it go faster.

stamina   the ability to work hard for a long time

taxes   money that you have to pay, in this case to a knight or lord

wits   the ability to think quickly

valiance   great courage

victor   winner

Index

armour 2, 3, 6, 8, 12–15, 18, 24, 25

castles 2, 6, 7, 21, 28

horses 2, 3, 5, 6, 9, 10, 14, 15, 18, 22, 24, 25

knights 2, 3, 4, 9, 10, 12, 14, 15–22, 24–26

ladies 4, 5, 7, 15, 16,

lords 4, 5, 17, 18, 20, 21, 29

practice 5, 7, 13

protect 16, 21, 22, 23

weapons 5, 6, 10, 11, 18, 25

Noble truth or fiendish falsehood? answers
p4: True; p14: True (but it is very expensive and only the richest knights can afford it); p19: True; p21: True; p24: False (although a full suit of armour could weigh up to 20kg!)

The knight's quiz answers
Mostly As? You'll never make it past a page.
Mostly Bs? You could be a reasonable squire.
Mostly Cs? You'll make a noble knight!